Gone Forever!

Tyrannosaurus

Rupert Matthews

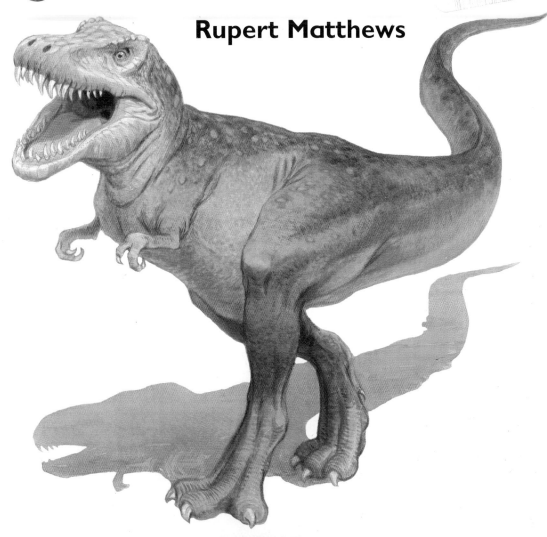

Heinemann LIBRARY

www.heinemann.co.uk/library
Visit our website to find out more information about Heinemann Library books.

To order:

Phone ++44 (0)1865 888066
Send a fax to ++44 (0)1865 314091
Visit the Heinemann Bookshop at www.heinemann.co.uk/library to browse our catalogue and
order online.

First published in Great Britain by Heinemann Library, Halley Court, Jordan Hill, Oxford OX2 8EJ, a part of Harcourt Education. Heinemann is a registered trademark of Harcourt Education Ltd.

Editorial: Andrew Farrow and Dan Nunn
Design: Ron Kamen and Paul Davies & Associates
Illustrations: Maureen and Gordon Gray, James Field (SGA) and Darren Lingard
Picture Research: Maria Joannou, Rebecca Sodergren and Frances Topp
Production: Viv Hichens
Originated by Anbassador Litho Ltd
Printed and bound in China by South China Printing Company

07 06 05 04 03   08 07 06 05 04
10 9 8 7 6 5 4 3 2 1   10 9 8 7 6 5 4 3 2 1
ISBN 0 431 16600 5   ISBN 0 431 16607 2
(hardback)   (paperback)

British Library Cataloguing in Publication Data

Matthews, Rupert
  Tyrannosaurus Rex. - (Gone forever)
  1. Tyrannosaurus rex - Juvenile literature
  I. Title
  567.9'129

Acknowledgements

The Publishers are grateful to the following for permission to reproduce photographs: Ardea/Francois Gohier pp. **4**, **12**, **22**, **24**; Corbis p. **14**; Field Museum, Chicago p. **26**; Geoscience Features Picture Library p. **6**; Natural History Museum, London pp. **8**, **18**, **20**; Science Photo Library p. **10**; Visuals Unlimited p. **16** (C. P. George).

Cover photo reproduced with permission of Corbis.

Our thanks to Dr David Norman and Dr Angela Milner for their assistance in the preparation of this book.

Every effort has been made to contact copyright holders of any material reproduced in this book. Any omissions will be rectified in subsequent printings if notice is given to the Publishers.

Disclaimer

Contents

Some words are shown in bold, **like this**.
You can find out what they mean by looking in the Glossary.

Gone forever!

Sometimes, all animals of one sort die. This means they become **extinct**. Scientists study extinct animals by digging for **fossils**. Fossils are the remains of living things that have been turned into rock.

About 68–65 million years ago, the animals on Earth were very different from those alive today. Most of the animals that lived then have become extinct. One of these animals was Tyrannosaurus rex.

Where did Tyrannosaurus rex live?

Geologists are scientists who study rocks and how they were formed. Geologists have studied rocks in which Tyrannosaurus rex **fossils** were found. They have used the rocks to find out about the area where the **dinosaur** lived.

Tyrannosaurus lived in areas that were usually warm and damp. There were lots of hills and valleys. There were also **volcanoes**, which **erupted** smoke and ash.

A land of trees

fossil of a leaf

Plants can be found as **fossils**, too. Fossil plants can tell us what plants grew in the places where Tyrannosaurus lived. Scientists can tell if the plants grew in hot or cold areas.

Tyrannosaurus lived in woods and forests where there were plenty of open spaces. Pine trees and ferns were like those that grow today. Other plants were very different. There were no grasses at all.

Living with Tyrannosaurus rex

As well as the **fossils** of **dinosaurs**, the fossils of smaller creatures are sometimes found, too. These tell us what different types of animals lived at the same time as Tyrannosaurus rex.

fossil of a snake

Small **mammals** lived amongst the plants. The mammals hunted insects. Birds flew through the sky. Flying **reptiles**, called **pterosaurs**, flew high overhead looking for food. Snakes slithered along the ground. **Lizards** ate plants or small animals.

What was Tyrannosaurus?

Fossils of Tyrannosaurus skeletons show what kind of animal it was. It walked on its **hind legs**, which were very strong. The tail was heavy enough to balance the body. Tyrannosaurus was about 12 metres long.

Tyrannosaurus rex was a very powerful animal. It was one of the largest meat-eaters that ever lived. It was so heavy that the ground probably shook when it walked. Tyrannosaurus weighed about 6 tonnes.

Baby Tyrannosaurus

Scientists have not found any Tyrannosaurus rex eggs. But fossils of baby **dinosaurs** of other big meat-eaters have been found. These show us what Tyrannosaurus babies might have looked like.

dinosaur eggs

The babies looked quite like adults but were smaller
and thinner. They probably stayed near the nest
and were fed by the mother. Later they learned
how to hunt for their own food.

Growing up

The **fossils** of some young **dinosaurs** similar
to Tyrannosaurus have been found. They show
that young animals were more **agile** and could
run faster than adults like the one above.

Some scientists think that young Tyrannosaurus may have hunted together. They probably hunted small creatures, such as lizards. By the time the young Tyrannosaurus were fully grown, they were strong enough to hunt alone.

On the move

Tyrannosaurus had strong and heavy legs and hips. It had powerful muscles for walking. The tail was used to provide balance. Swishing its tail helped Tyrannosaurus rex to change direction quickly.

Scientists believe Tyrannosaurus walked slowly most of the time. It could run quite quickly when it wanted to. But Tyrannosaurus would have got tired quickly and could not run fast for long distances.

Designed to bite

Scientists have found many Tyrannosaurus teeth. Each tooth was up to 20 centimetres long and was very sharp. The edges of the teeth were jagged like steak knives.

Tyrannosaurus had dozens of teeth in its jaws. These teeth were able to tear through meat easily. This means Tyrannosaurus ate other **dinosaurs**. It used its teeth to bite off chunks of meat and crush bone.

Hunting

Some scientists believe Tyrannosaurus hunted for food. Tyrannosaurus could open its mouth very wide, then snap it shut with powerful muscles. This could have killed its **prey** with a single bite.

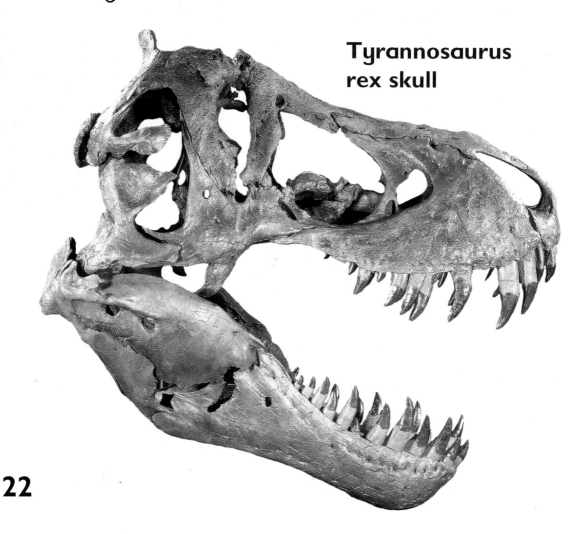

Tyrannosaurus rex skull

Tyrannosaurus could not run fast for very long.
It probably hid in trees or bushes and waited for
another **dinosaur** to come close. Then
Tyrannosaurus would dash out to attack its victim.

What did Tyrannosaurus eat?

Tyrannosaurus ate other **dinosaurs**, such as **hadrosaurs**. Hadrosaurs were large plant-eating dinosaurs. Some hadrosaur bones have been found with marks on them made by Tyrannosaurus teeth.

skeleton of a hadrosaur

Hadrosaurs were not as large or as strong as
Tyrannosaurus rex. They could be killed quite
easily, as long as they did not run off first.
Dozens of hadrosaur **fossils** have been found with
Tyrannosaurus fossils. This means that they lived
at the same time and in the same places.

Finding dead animals

Some scientists believe Tyrannosaurus did not hunt other **dinosaurs**. Most hunting dinosaurs used their front legs to grab hold of victims. Tyrannosaurus had tiny front legs. It might not have been a good hunter.

Perhaps Tyrannosaurus fed on large dinosaurs that had died of old age or disease. Tyrannosaurus could probably smell a dead dinosaur from a long way away. Then it would come to feast on the body.

Tyrannosaurus around the world

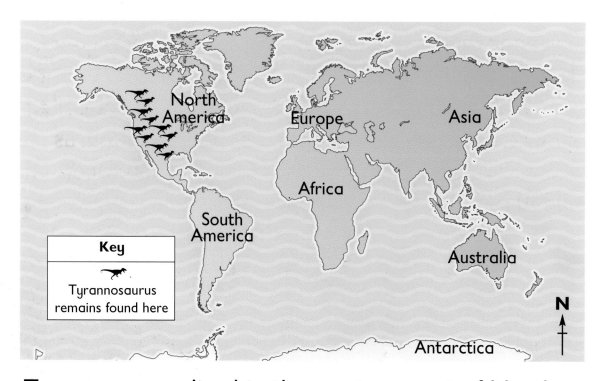

Tyrannosaurus lived in the western part of North America. It did not reach eastern areas because the centre of the continent was covered by a large, shallow sea at the time. Other **dinosaurs** similar to Tyrannosaurus lived several million years earlier in North America and in East Asia.

When did Tyrannosaurus live?

Tyrannosaurus existed for just a few million years. It lived at the very end of the Age of the Dinosaurs, about 65 million years ago (mya). Dinosaurs called Albertosaurus, Tarbosaurus and Daspletosaurus were very similar to Tyrannosaurus. They lived slightly earlier.

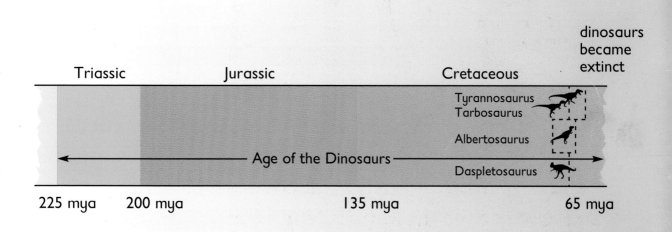

dinosaurs became extinct

Triassic   Jurassic   Cretaceous

Tyrannosaurus
Tarbosaurus

Albertosaurus

← Age of the Dinosaurs

Daspletosaurus

225 mya   200 mya   135 mya   65 mya

Fact file

Tyrannosaurus rex	
Length:	up to 12 metres
Height:	up to 6 metres
Weight:	6 tonnes
When it lived:	Late Cretaceous Period, about 65 million years ago
Where it lived:	North America

How to say it

dinosaur – dine-oh-saw
hadrosaur – had-row-saw

pterosaur – tear-oh-saw
Tyrannosaurus rex – Tie-ran-oh-saw-rus recks

Glossary

agile able to run quickly, jump about and change direction easily

dinosaur one of a large group of extinct reptiles that lived on land. Dinosaurs lived on Earth between 225 and 65 million years ago.

erupt to burst out, like the lava and ash coming from a volcano

extinct an animal is extinct when there are none of its kind left alive

fossil remains of a plant or animal, usually found in rocks. Sometimes the remains have been turned into rock. Most fossils are bones or teeth because these hard parts are more easily preserved. Some fossils are traces of animals, such as their footprints.

hadrosaurs types of large plant-eating dinosaurs which lived at the same time as the Tyrannosaurus

hind legs back legs of an animal

lizard small reptile with four legs

mammal animal with hair or fur. Mammals give birth to live young instead of laying eggs.

prey animals which are killed and eaten by another animal

pterosaur type of extinct reptile. It had wings made of skin and could fly. There were many different sorts of pterosaur.

reptile cold-blooded animal, such as a modern snake or lizard

volcano opening in the Earth's surface where hot rocks, lava and ash come out

Find out more

These are some books about dinosaurs:
Big Book of Dinosaurs, Angela Wilkes (Dorling Kindersley, 2001)
Pop-up and Pull Out T-Rex, David Hawcock
  (Dorling Kindersley, 2001)
Dinosaur Park, Nick Denchfield (Macmillan, 1998)

Look at these websites for more information:
www.oink.demon.co.uk/topics/dinosaur.htm
www.enchantedlearning.com/subjects/dinos
www.fmnh.org/sue/

Index